Treasure of Words

Book 4 Reflections of God Moments

56 One Minute Devotionals

Dedication

Treasured words and knowledge come from a wealth of understanding and experience. This book is dedicated with honor to all of the pastors and teachers who have shown the love of truth from the Word of God into the life of this author. I am blessed to have learned and gleaned at the feet of Jesus and had shepherds of faith who guided me in the process of learning from youth to adulthood.

Written by: Donesa Walker
Design by: Will Baten

Table of Contents:

1. Lord, Bless You

2. Word-filled Death

3. Lifted

4. Live in Me

5. Step on His Toes

6. Harvest

7. Exhale the Light

8. The Simplicity

9. Blameless

10. Wages

11. Labor Rewarded

12. Written in Past

13. First Pray

14. Battered

15. Timely Assurance

16. Accessories

17. Perfected Love

18. Mercy Stays

19. A Good Name

20. Every Knee

21. But Now

22. The Treasure

23. Cease to Stray

24. Caught Up

25. Do You Believe This?

26. Near Enough

27. Rumors

28. Grounded

29. Living Word

30. A Lot

31. He Was and IS…

32. GPS

33. Heavy Rest

34. Prepare the Heart

35. Adventures

36. All Knowing

37. Focus

38. Salt n Light

39. Anxiety

40. Got IT

41. Tall orders

42. What is the Light of Life?

43. Rejoice

44. Ouch!

45. Eye of God

46. Born of Spirit

47. Earth

48. Hustle

49. Anchored

50. My Processing

51. The Promise

52. The Semicolon

53. Blame Game

54. The Part

55. Guided Counsel

56. Longest Chapter

May the Lord answer you in the day of trouble;
May the name of the God of Jacob defend you;
May He send you help from the sanctuary, And
strengthen you out of Zion; May He remember all
your offerings, And accept your burnt sacrifice.
Selah May He grant you according to your heart's
desire, And fulfill all your purpose. We will rejoice
in your salvation, And in the name of our God we
will set up our banners!
May the Lord fulfill all your petitions.
Now I know that the Lord saves His anointed; He
will answer him from His holy heaven with the
saving strength of His right hand. Some trust
in chariots, and some in horses; But we will remember the name of the Lord our God. They have
bowed down and fallen; But we have risen and
stand upright. Save, Lord!
May the King answer us when we call.

Psalms 20:1-9

Lord, Bless You

A comma is a little thing that changes meaning in speech just like attitude towards others changes your perspectives. Over time we look at things through various lenses. What was once a hard thing can become something nostalgic or an embarrassment can become a thing of laughter...even sorrow can become sweeter with time. But time doesn't change everything, it doesn't change the situation but rather the perspective to the situation. David's song of blessing here is meant to direct the mind towards seeing His purpose. At the time he wrote, people who had wealth and power demonstrated it with the best horses and fastest chariots much like those today do with houses and cars. His blessing is not about wealth and power but something much more valuable...God's favor.

He is saying that when we raise our banners of praise to God instead of men then God's responsiveness to us is the reward. I sit here listening to the birds calling to one another as I watch the river eddy and flow teaming with life. I've watched the day dawn and as the fog burned away, the perspective changed. The view became clearer. Often, we get caught up in watching the horses and chariots of others and trusting in that vision when God has so much more for us if we would just take some time to wait on Him which changes our perspective. He's such a good God patiently waiting for us to allow the fog of life that is clouding our vision to give us His vision. Taste and see that God is good. His mercies are new every morning and great is His faithfulness. Press into His perspective. God, keep your perspective clear.

"You're familiar with the command to the ancients, 'Do not murder.' I'm telling you that anyone who is so much as angry with a brother or sister is guilty of murder. Carelessly call a brother 'idiot!' and you just might find yourself hauled into court. Thoughtlessly yell 'stupid!' at a sister and you are on the brink of hellfire. The simple moral fact is that words kill.

Matthew 5:21-22

Word-Filled Death

All the armchair experts are weighing in on tragedy using it to drive their agenda forward...making words their weapon to kill and destroy others without a care that this is just as serious as the tragedy itself. In Matthew, Jesus is teaching on the seriousness of the words of law that have consequences then states clearly that hating and anger is just as punishable morally as murder. The fact is that careless, unintentional words kill often just as much as an evil person with a weapon. I see children walk into my office every day who have been completely destroyed in their psyche by the careless words of others. My love language is words of affirmation, so I have experienced "word death" of more than one relationship in my life but even though I have experienced it myself and try to be cautious, sometimes I carelessly hurl "word weapons" that harm others out of frustration and this is not ok. Marriages, relationships, working cultures and individuals have been healed or destroyed by words. I've watched "word bombs" being hurled in anger and dodged them myself.

I've seen the utter devastation left behind "word hurricanes". God has called us to issue "word balm" through dispensing His love not to wreak havoc through our own "word weapons". When my brother was murdered, and I use that word because there was intent behind his death...my family was reeling but I'll never forget the "word land mine" that hit our family from someone close as they hurled hateful sentiment from a complete lack of knowledge of who God is. The thing about "word bombs" is that although you can apologize and add "word balm" through love, the wound takes time to heal and is tender to the person for a while. The more direct exposure or repetitive hits from these they've had, the more likely the emotional damage is wrought. Millions if not billions of dollars are spent each year in therapy to counsel people who have been exposed to these carelessly and now with social media being so available, these words are bouncing and ricocheting around being added to by others and gaining momentum which continues to destroy. Jesus' words themselves are taken and bent, used in an evil manner by others but God's promise is so true that His words will not return void.

Words kill and words give life, hope and balm. How are we using our words? Begin to speak life. If you are exhausted and cannot believe anymore...begin to pray his words of life over your word battered heart...pray songs, pray His words...the balm of His love will begin to heal, bring hope -and restore.

I can't wait to hear what he'll say.
God's about to pronounce his people well,
The holy people he loves so much,
so they'll never again live like fools.
See how close his salvation is to those who fear him?
Our country is home base for Glory!
Love and Truth meet in the street,
Right Living and Whole Living embrace and kiss!
Truth sprouts green from the ground,
Right Living pours down from the skies!
Oh yes! God gives Goodness and Beauty;
our land responds with Bounty and Blessing.
Right Living strides out before him,
and clears a path for his passage.

PSALM 85:8-13

Lifted

So... well, to those who follow closely...I obviously didn't post this morning. I woke up so refreshed by His word, made my scripture pictures...then my day tilted sideways...the spirit of doubt and I am not enough kicked in and I allowed it! I began a frustrating time of whoa is me...not that I let anyone know...well...they knew I was frustrated...but God, in His loving way...put someone into my day! He does that. He allowed His love and His truth to crash into my life with a hug! A hug I needed so badly. A person who spoke joy and blessing into my life just by being herself! She poured God's love into my spirit and reset my stinkin' thinkin' that was going on...that's who God is! I was walking into the door of my office allowing the pressures of life to weigh me down when suddenly He called my name through a friend's voice...He hugged me through my friend's arms...He restored me with an embrace and truth sprouted up...I am certainly not enough but I can do all things through Christ who strengthens me! Thank you, my sister, in the Lord for following your impulse and being the hands of God extended! I cannot wait to see what He does next.... that one moment poured into me allowing me to sense Him and be able to pour into others today!

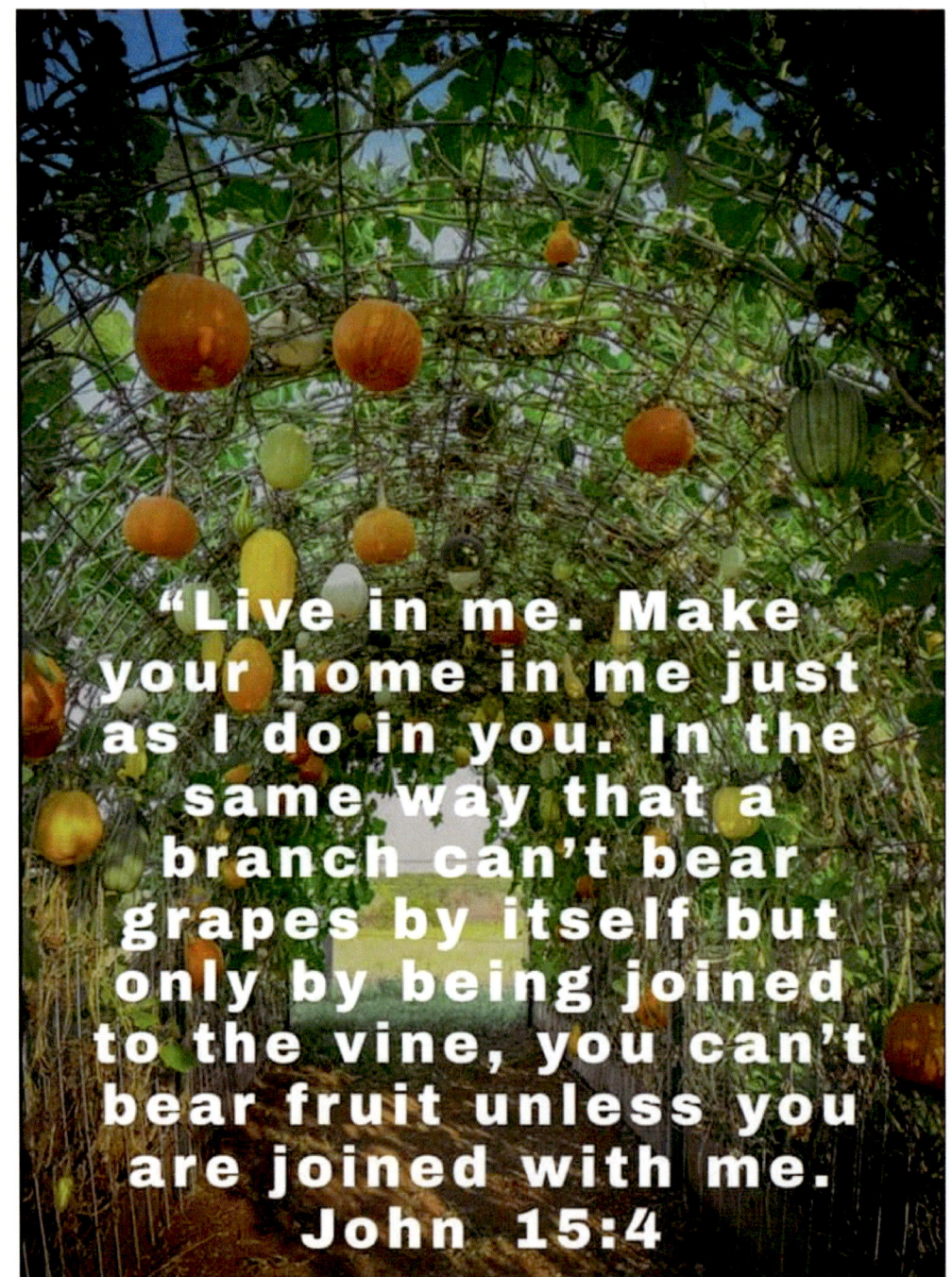

"Live in me. Make your home in me just as I do in you. In the same way that a branch can't bear grapes by itself but only by being joined to the vine, you can't bear fruit unless you are joined with me.
John 15:4

Live in me

I've read this verse/chapter so many times and yet each time, God speaks about it to me a little differently. I always perceived the first two sentences as emphasis rather than two fully different meanings. I got my puppies a new doggy bed...they like it, the jump into it...and they sleep or wallow in it but the difference is that my oldest dog makes his home in it...he moves it around, fluffs it like he wants it and preps it so it's just right..,the point is...you can live somewhere and it not be your home...your spirit isn't settled there...I know. We moved to the lake years ago and the home was gorgeous, and it was my house, I lived there. But it was never my home.

My spirit never settled there...probably because it was too far, and I wasn't there much but I lived there four years without it being my home, only being my house....do you see what I am saying. Your home is where your spirit settles, it provides nourishment to you, it feeds your soul.... God is telling us not to just settle in Him and go about the motions but to truly take Him in... breathe in Him, fuel in Him, let your spirit breathe in His Spirit...allowing Him to become your home! I love this picture because it shows how the framework is there and the vine had settled, weaved, and become attached to the framework so much that the fruit is dependent on the branches/vine and held in place by the framework. Don't let life make you feel all alone! Settle in. He's there living in you now you just need to get busy nesting in Him. Take Him in for He longs for you.

You're blessed when you stay on course, walking steadily on the road revealed by God. You're blessed when you follow his directions, doing your best to find him. That's right—you don't go off on your own; you walk straight along the road he set. You, God, prescribed the right way to live; now you expect us to live it. Oh, that my steps might be steady, keeping to the course you set; Then I'd never have any regrets in comparing my life with your counsel. I thank you for speaking straight from your heart; I learn the pattern of your righteous ways. I'm going to do what you tell me to do; don't ever walk off and leave me.

Psalm 119:1-8

Step on His Toes

I added this to my story this morning and I walked in it all day...today, I saw a little boy step on his daddy's toes of his boots and grab his hands...then as the dad walked, the boy was held securely mimicking the dad's pattern, learning his stride but safe on his feet...it was beautiful and shouted this verse back to me...then tonight as some friends were over with their puppy..I watched him trying his best to engage my dogs in play away from their routine...they are too set in their patterns so that they held steady...much to his disappointment. Again, I felt this verse reverberate. The blessings of God come from walking the steady course that He reveals as we do our very best to follow His lead...Even when the path seems obscured by trials, loss, pain, disappointment, and so much other...we know His patterns...we've learned His stride and when the road gets too hard to walk, just step up on His boots...and put your hands in His and let His love & character carry you along..,

Don't be misled: No one makes a fool of God. What a person plants, he will harvest. The person who plants selfishness, ignoring the needs of others—ignoring God!—harvests a crop of weeds. All he'll have to show for his life is weeds! But the one who plants in response to God, letting God's Spirit do the growth work in him, harvests a crop of real life, eternal life.

Galatians 6:7-8

Harvest

The harvest moon is out tonight reminding us that it is time for the harvest. It's time for God's laborers to step up and out. The harvest is rich, but the laborers are few, so it is time to pray to our God, the God of the harvest that He call those to Him who are willing to work the fields because they are ripe for harvest. What a person plants, he harvests. If we plant service to others, we will be served. If we plant kindness, we will reap kindness, if we plant hate, then we will reap violence. If we are selfish and ignore God, then we harvest a crop of weeds that do nothing for us but cause grief. If we choose to plant in response to what God is calling forth in us, we will gain a harvest of eternal life. No one makes a fool of God or gets one over on Him. He sees us all in our good and bad. We will harvest from the things we invest in daily. If we invest only in our own wants and desires, then we will harvest that worthless crop. While it may look like it is worthwhile here, there is no life in it and so it will fade and die, withering under the sun as our bodies age and our wealth is eaten away.

Don't burn out; keep yourselves fueled and aflame. Be alert servants of the Master, cheerfully expectant. Don't quit in hard times; pray all the harder. Help needy Christians; be inventive in hospitality.

Romans 12:11-13

Exhale the Light

Somedays are just exhausting...and you feel burned out, tired and worn down. These are the days where you need to dig a little deeper into The Lord and allow Him to reignite you. The last two years have been exhausting in the media, the political front and in the stress of daily life.... if your focus stays on these things, you will feel like quitting. This verse instructs us...to keep alert and aflame. It tells us to press in and pray harder...if you continue to read, it says your adversary is going about as a roaring lion seeking whom he may devour...but remember that God closed the mouths of the lions when Daniel prayed. It's time that we be creative in our outreach to share the love of Jesus. A flame ignites the fuel around it...catch a spark of Jesus calling you.... go light your world!

But what does it say? "The word is near you, in your mouth and in your heart (that is, the word of faith which we preach): that if you confess with your mouth the Lord Jesus and believe in your heart that God has raised Him from the dead, you will be saved. For with the heart one believes unto righteousness, and with the mouth confession is made unto salvation.

Romans 10:8-10

The Simplicity

The simplicity salvation is what baffles the unbeliever. How can we simply say we believe and be saved? The Word. Notice that the phrase says; "believes unto righteousness"...this means that we are joining the faith walk...think of the men walking along the road to Emmaus with Jesus, talking about Him and all that was done but failing to recognize the truth to have been with them and in their presence the whole time...what a shock when He revealed what they failed to see. This is the same with us. The Word (Jesus) is near you, in your mouth and in your heart...The Word of Faith but you must recognize Him. You must acknowledge Him. You must become in tune with Him to hear his voice. I think of my life as a radio and His word as the tune button that allows me to tweak the channel until His voice is clear, present, and loud in my life. Sometimes I'm out of tune. For some people they still have the radio but don't turn it on. Or they turn it on and only hear static because they don't take the time to tune it. Just imagine if the wise mean didn't seek the star, follow the charts...imagine if the scientists studying the heavens didn't fine tune their instruments...they would be wrong, deceived, led astray...as many in science are right now...making science into what they want it to say...this is what happens to us when we try to tune the word away from The Word and into our own meanings. "For with the heart one believes unto righteousness".... this means if you allow The Word (Jesus) who is near you to be tuned into your heart through faith then He will be in you (in your heart) speak through you (in your mouth) and guide you (in faith). Get away from the static of this world and tune into your Creator, the Lover of your soul. Time to change that channel and begin a new walk!

Do all things without complaining and disputing, that you may become blameless and harmless, children of God without fault in the midst of a crooked and perverse generation, among whom you shine as lights in the world,

Philippians 2:14-15

Blameless

Today is a day to recognize our sons and a couple of days ago it was National Daughter's Day, so on this National Son's Day, I think it only right that we acknowledge that we are heirs to a kingdom...we are sons and daughters of the king and this comes with responsibilities....we are charged to do whatever our hands find to do with all our heart, soul, mind & strength as unto God without complaining and disputes. What? The church must agree together. This is why and where Satan has gotten his strength...when a cord is wound together with many strands, it is not easily broken but when the cord is raveled by wear, stress, and not cared for so that the mice and pests get to chewing on it...well, it's not strong. How do we strengthen our own walk and those around us? How do we become blameless and harmless in the midst of this crooked and perverse society? We do all things as unto God. This is tough. A while back, a fad or trend went around called WWJD....the message was correct but because the actions were not implemented with the mind of God in charge, it faded quickly. This mindset is what Christ wanted not this bickering mindset we have now. How do we overcome this argumentative mindset? By putting all things through the lens of God's purpose. Let's be clear...this is a journey, and no one is perfect at it except Christ Jesus, but we can and should strive to be like Him.

Do all things doesn't mean you do all that you are told by a wicked government either; it means you do the work of God without complaining and bickering. God and Government are not always in line. When you choose to follow God, you choose to follow His leading over that of any other. Wait...isn't that contrary to scripture...not at all...His words are to do all things through prayer and supplication so that your labor be not in vain... if it aligns with His purpose that you have ascertained through prayer and reading and perhaps Godly counsel... then do what He directs you to do. Why do some Christians feel one way about something, and others feel another? Honestly, I know the mind of God isn't divided. All I can say is that I seek Him with all my heart. Do I fail? Yes, I'm human but when I fail...I know He will forgive me if I ask with a contrite, sincere heart. Lord, help me to stand as a light among the darkness of this present world. A beacon on a hill that others may see. Please forgive me for my failures and direct my path with your word, light & love. Today help me to do all that you put before me without complaining and with joy as I see it as a ministry unto you.

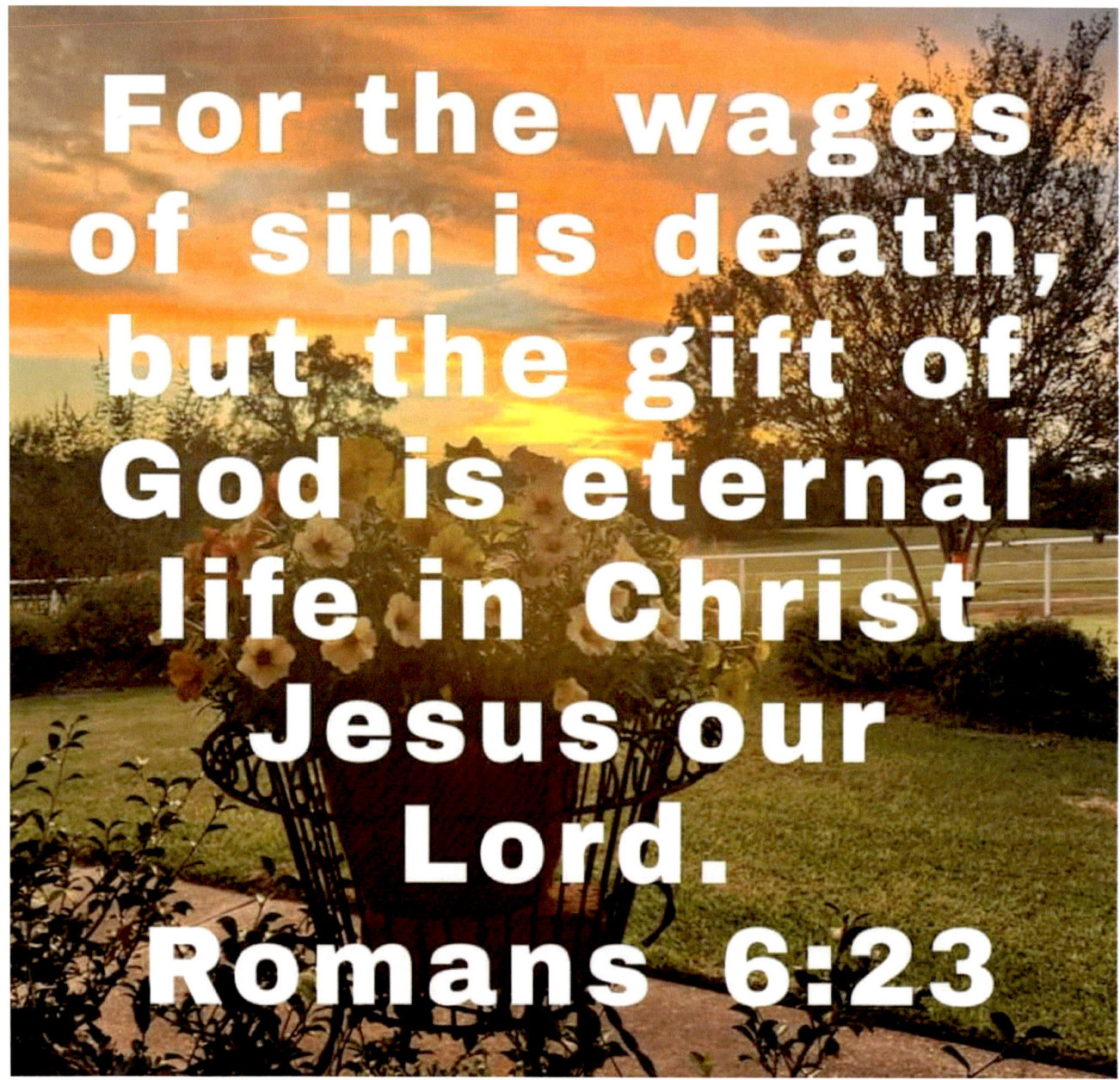

For the wages of sin is death, but the gift of God is eternal life in Christ Jesus our Lord. Romans 6:23

Wages

A friend posted this beautiful picture of the sunset, and I thought what a bucolic setting. Such a reward at the end of the day. Which led me to realize this morning that this is where our mindset should be...at the end of the journey in the world. The Jeopardy version...eternal hope.... for $$$eternal life...forever.... what are the wages of our current existence? The thing is...many who profess to be Christians have a "If I can just get through today, my reward is Heaven" approach. That's so sad because you aren't walking in Eternal Hope. The gift of God is eternal life IN Christ Jesus.... that's now. Yes, we have eternal hope for Heavenly reward but the now is the walk with Christ...this is the gift you don't have to wait for...I see some of you didn't get that...when I labor or work, it isn't in vain or as a waste of time...I am doing all He puts before me With Him! IN Him! This is the gift. Let's try it a third time because when you get it, you'll be rejoicing...your payment for the Christian walk is that you get to walk in the Steps of the Master, in His power/authority...you have His power of attorney, His checkbook of faith, you are IN Him for His peace, His love, His protection, His promises, His joy, His all in all, His constant presence...IN HIM!!! Why aren't you opening the gift? Using His gifts? His spirit is here to provide for you, hold you up, be your everything...there is an eternal reward that is fabulous but there is absolutely no need to walk in a downtrodden fashion when He has sent His spirit to dwell in you an empower you right now as His gift! Thank you, Lord, for giving me a song in my heart- a melody to play in this walk!

Two are better than one, Because they have a good reward for their labor.

Ecclesiastes 4:9

Labor Rewarded

In Ecclesiastes, King Solomon is writing from the wisdom God has given him and he instructs that two are better than one.... giving many examples of this and even adding that a three-cord strand is not easily broken. I've heard this a lot and even seen beautiful depictions at weddings and songs about this, but I never really observed the because.... Because is a word that tells you about the cause behind the being of the previous statement.... These two are better because THEY have a good reward for their labor meaning that two receive more pay than one if both work. In all the beautiful ceremonies I've seen and all the songs I've heard.... never has anyone addressed this. It's important. When two become one in marriage, if one of the two carries the load and responsibility in anything then that reward is lesser than if both contributed to it. Does this mean you have to be married to enjoy life? Not at all. It is simply expressing that when two are involved in a labor of any kind, the reward is more...let me take it spiritual for a minute...if two pray together then see results, both see the power of that prayer...if two pray together and see no results, both still feel the power of that prayer and have the accountability to keep praying together...the point here is that pulling together lessens the load and increases the rewards whether it be in life, marriage or in spiritual matters.

Join someone today and enjoy your day!

For everything that was written in the past was written to teach us, so that through the endurance taught in the Scriptures and the encouragement they provide we might have hope.

Romans 15:4

Written in Past

𝄞 "Troublesome times are here, filling men's heart with fear, freedoms we all hold dear now are at stake. Humbling our hearts to God, safe from His chastening rod, seek the way Pilgrims trod. Christians AWAKE!! Jesus is coming soon...morning or night or noon!"

This is an old song with very apt words...like the words in Scripture, it was written to encourage us to endure through to the end. Hope. Eternal Hope-the rapture of the church, the catching away of the bride is getting ever closer....but a time of trying is coming first in which each of us will cry out how much longer God.., a time of yearning...a time of endurance...this may look different for each one of us but it is here...no matter what happens...false accusations to trying of the spirit/body....he or she that endures through to the end holding onto hope in Christ Jesus will have eternal life.

𝄞 "Our hope is built on nothing less, than Jesus' blood & righteousness. I dare not trust the sweetest frame but only trust in Jesus' name. Christ alone, cornerstone, weak becomes strong in the Savior's love. Through the storms, He is Lord...Lord of ALL! "

Make this your common practice: Confess your sins to each other and pray for each other so that you can live together whole and healed. The prayer of a person living right with God is something powerful to be reckoned with. Elijah, for instance, human just like us, prayed hard that it wouldn't rain, and it didn't—not a drop for three and a half years. Then he prayed that it would rain, and it did. The showers came and everything started growing again.

James 5:16-18

First Pray

My confession...I often forget that my first go to should be prayer. I had so many people say to me that they wish they could do something more than pray...but, the truth is that if we acted in prayer with the power & authority that Jesus gave us (think power of attorney) then we, through prayer are more powerful than anything on earth. The prayer of one man living right with God caused rain not to come for years...until he prayed and believed that it would come again. This means the best thing and first thing you should do in a situation is pray. Through prayer, Lions' mouths were sealed, waters separated, blind could see, deaf could hear...miracle after miracle...the same God who raised Lazarus from the grave lives in us and if we tap into His Authority and pray in His righteousness.... dwelling in Him... we have power to command a mountain to be thrown into the sea. I pray today that our spiritual eyes be awakened to know and understand His will fully in our lives so that we can begin to walk boldly in His authority!

Let the word of Christ dwell in you richly in all wisdom, teaching and admonishing one another in psalms and hymns and spiritual songs, singing with grace in your hearts to the Lord.

Colossians 3:16

Battered

Speaking to a friend earlier today and we discussed how the fabric of life has been torn between families and friends, churches, coworkers, and throughout our world. When this Scripture says let the word of Christ dwell in you...it's speaking about The Word! Let Christ live in you. Not just in you but in you Richly. Richness in life isn't about monetary means or goods...richness in life is the Grace of God. It's a gift that knows no boundaries. People are flawed, they are tattered and torn much like palm trees after a hurricane, but if the life blood of Grace which comes from the rooted source of Christ is allowed to flow in you, then the storms may batter one about without causing the life to be shorn. So how does Christ dwell in me? In wisdom, teaching, correction, singing, and in GRACE! His word is our life blood. it gives us wisdom to stay rooted, teaches us how to move in the winds of life without being blown over, prunes us through the storms and results in beautiful melodies of life as the wind of God blows through us. Like a tree planted by water, when we are rooted in Christ, the storms of life simply are a melody that plays darkly, richly, sweetly, and blessedly. No matter what your task today...allow the word of Christ to whisper Grace through the circumstances. Thank you Lord for the richness of life in the word.

I will lift up my eyes to the hills– From whence comes my help? My help comes from the Lord, Who made heaven and earth. He will not allow your foot to be moved;He who keeps you will not slumber. Behold, He who keeps Israel Shall neither slumber nor sleep. The Lord is your keeper; The Lord is your shade at your right hand. The sun shall not strike you by day, Nor the moon by night. The Lord shall preserve you from all evil; He shall preserve your soul. The Lord shall preserve your going out and your coming in From this time forth, and even forevermore.

Psalms 121:1-8

Timely Assurance

What a wonderful promise and timely assurance! Interesting that David says I will lift my eyes.... why? He says I'll lift my eyes to tell us that He will get out of his own way and trust God. Lifting your eye to the hills means you gotta look up and refocus your vision from the step-by-step monotonous moment of self. He is reminding us that our help isn't in our own hand alone but in God who made all of heaven and earth. He will hold you so that you don't sink and be your back while you rest. This assurance comes from a man who was on the run for his life in the wilderness from a powerful king seeking to destroy him because God had chosen him over the king and anointed him through Samuel. Saul had gotten into a bad state of mind wrapped up in his own power and privilege...and he was acting erratically. The Spirit of God had departed from him, and Saul was self absorbed and power hungry. Reminds me so much of where we are today with the Spirit of God not operating in our government and the people in charge who are money grabbing, power hungry and evil. They have become lovers of themselves, and self-absorbed as God describes in Revelation. David reminds us that in our moments of struggle, terror, and frustration...our help comes from God. We are to look to Him! He is our source. In this setting, a soldier had to use his shield in his right hand to cover him from the enemy as well as the sun and rain.

David is reminding us that God is our shield...our source...our protector...our keeper, and that He watches over us constantly as He doesn't need sleep, so He doesn't falter in His care nor slumber...what a powerful reminder. Isn't it time we gave the burden over to Him and trusted His care? This chapter ends with the assurance of legacy. David says he watches our going out and coming in forever, assuring our legacy. Not infamy...legacy. That means God is watching and planning our future even while He protects, guards, and directs our present. Take a moment and look up from your situation to God and let Him take control. He's got this!

Let not mercy and truth forsake you;
Bind them around your neck, Write
them on the tablet of your heart, And
so find favor and high esteem In the
sight of God and man.
Proverbs 3:3-4

Accessories

I put a necklace on most every day, but today as I put my necklace on...I thought of God's mercy and truth as my accessories. Why do we wear accessories? To speak to others before we meet them...to endorse us... to enhance our appearance and confidence...just imagine if each morning you bound your neck with truth and mercy...if you let truth and mercy speak before you as you enter a room...the word tells us that by writing truth and mercy upon the tablets of our heart (because out of the abundance of the heart, the mouth speaks) then we would find favor & high esteem with God and man! So... let's try some Truth & Mercy today. Tell the truth, share The Truth (Jesus is the Way, The Truth, The Life) ...give mercy today...Mercy rewrote my life...God's mercy...every time I've fallen...He has given me His mercy when I should've been judged...let's try some mercy for others given through The Truth!

Love has been perfected among us in this: that we may have boldness in the day of judgment; because as He is, so are we in this world. There is no fear in love; but perfect love casts out fear, because fear involves torment. But he who fears has not been made perfect in love. We love Him because He first loved us.

I John 4:17-19

Perfected Love

October is Breast Cancer Awareness Month and a celebration each year in my heart as it is the anniversary of the conquering of fear. In July 2015, my mom was diagnosed with stage 4 breast cancer, and I got scared. I began to pray as I had never prayed before. I interceded, I researched, I worshipped, I spent time with mom & God. I watched this woman of faith walk through this terrible journey without a moment of fear...with complete peace and I learned what perfect love really was all about. Perfect love...the kind only God gives really does cast out fear. I watched 2020 unfold as the year that Fear took the reigns of life from many people, but I have never feared in this time because I learned this lesson in 2015. So, what's the secret? Boldness. Boldness that as He is... so we are. Let me say that so you really get it! God has already walked this human frame in the life of Jesus...he walked it to know our mindsets and He conquered death, hell and the grave. If we love Him then there is no fear of death. There is no fear of life. There is no fear because it cannot exist in the light of his love just like darkness cannot exist in light. Love has been perfected through boldness to approach Him with our concerns knowing that He is faithful and just. He gives us the power to move these mountains whether by the shovel or the bulldozer or by an earthquake that reduces them to rubble. Fear cannot stay any longer...because His perfect love has cast it out and it is His will that mine & your life be healed! Hallelujah! Celebrate in His perfect love! Allow Him to fill you with peace! His healing is perfect whether here or in eternity! That's the secret., no more fear! Perfect peace!

For the mountains shall depart And the hills be removed, But My kindness shall not depart from you, Nor shall My covenant of peace be removed," Says the Lord, who has mercy on you.

Isaiah 54:10

Mercy Stays

We admire the mountains and hills as a thing of creation with permanence, but God is saying to us through this verse that His peace, kindness, and mercy have more foundation than these mountains. Dwell on that for a minute. Think of what foundation you have built your hopes upon. My hope is built on nothing less than Jesus' blood and righteousness. We dare not trust any man, government nor political party. We cannot put our faith in any individual or group. Foundations are built on a strong cornerstone that doesn't shift with the sands beneath.... they are dug deep into layers of earth so that slight shifts won't crack the foundation. What are you basing your life on? Are you trusting in the sands of government which is blown about by every wind of change? Make sure your faith is set solidly upon God's word. Go to the source. Trust only His leading, calling and direction. Remember He is a mountain moving God.

A good name is better than precious ointment, And the day of death than the day of one's birth; Wisdom is good with an inheritance, And profitable to those who see the sun. For wisdom is a defense as money is a defense, But the excellence of knowledge is that wisdom gives life to those who have it. Wisdom strengthens the wise More than ten rulers of the city. I applied my heart to know, To search and seek out wisdom and the reason of things, To know the wickedness of folly, Even of foolishness and madness.

Ecclesiastes 7:1, 11-12, 19, 25

A Good Name

Wisdom. Excellence of knowledge. Reason of Things.
Solomon spoke from his gift of Wisdom that a good name is better than precious ointment which was very costly in his time. Wisdom as a defense is better than money. Wisdom gives life to those who have excellence of knowledge and strengthens the wise more than the authorities in government power. He advises us to seek out wisdom and the reason for things. Wisdom...good as an inheritance...and with an inheritance...are you gifting your kids with wisdom by how/who you seek knowledge from in your life. Are they gaining wisdom from your actions and deeds? What legacy of wisdom are you leaving behind you. If your legacy is one of wealth and not wisdom, that will surely be burnt up in only hours. Wisdom....I was reading just this morning that 1 point in IQ is equivalent to just over $14,290 over a lifetime. Wonder what wisdom is worth? Scripture tells us that it is more valuable than rubies. Wisdom...a priceless gift...

And every creature which is in heaven and on the earth and under the earth and such as are in the sea, and all that are in them, I heard saying: "Blessing and honor and glory and power Be to Him who sits on the throne, And to the Lamb, forever and ever!"

Revelation 5:13

Every Knee

EVERY knee will bow and everything on the earth and in the heavens will acknowledge that He is Lord. Wrap your brain around this! EVERYTHING acknowledges that He is Lord. I look at the beauty of nature and think how anyone could not acknowledge it. The lust for power corrupts even that which at one time was sacred. Lucifer himself had the attention of God himself and yet rejected it in his lust for power. But in that great and powerful day, every single atom, molecule, virus, being, etc....shall acknowledge that He, the Lamb who was slain at the foundation of the world, is God of all. Nature cries it out even now. All things under the sun are subject to the power of His name. Grasp it. Why would we get so wrapped up in what could be when we know what is? Why do we worry and fret when we know the Creator of all mankind? And the question is... "And yet, What is man that thou art mindful of him?" God created you with the sole purpose of worshiping Him, walking with Him, fellowshipping with Him. Are you living up to your purpose? Are you acknowledging Him in all you do, say, are? He's coming soon!

But now, o Lord, You are our Father;
We are the clay, and You our potter;
And all we are the work of
Your hand.

Isaiah 64:8

But Now

What a wondrous creator! The beautiful mountains, streams, and valleys...and what is man? God created us from clay...from the very molecular structure of the earth and we are the works of His hands.... marvel at that....

The same hands that formed the mountains and the rivers made you. The same hands that made the stars and moon created you. The same word that spoke Light into being formed us. But only man is God breathed. All other in creation was created and formed by God but only mankind is God breathed. He formed man then breathed the breath of life into him. That will boggle your mind if you think about it. Only mankind has the very essence of God breathed into us. We are the work of His hand, formed under the word of His voice and breathe the very air that He breathed into us. Wow!

"The lamp of the body is the eye. If therefore your eye is good, your whole body will be full of light. But if your eye is bad, your whole body will be full of darkness. If therefore the light that is in you is darkness, how great is that darkness!

Matthew 6:22-23

The Treasure

Treasures. Yesterday as I stood atop Pike's Peak and looked at all my eye could behold, I marveled at the work of God's hands. When I tried to capture that beautiful scene in photos, I found it lacking. Photos do not do justice to the marvel of creation. As I listened to the tour guide explain about the richness of gold in the hills and how millions of dollars in gold are taken every day from these hills...The treasury is full in the earth and men toil and scrape to find the gold, capture the moment, and live for the thrill. But God, the creator of all said the streets of heaven are made from that which we treasure here...what is filling the light of your eyes? If you are more concerned with taking care of your bank account than the child starving in the street, then your treasure will rust or be stolen. No one takes into eternity that which he saves here on earth. The future is filled with what you have sown because that is what you will harvest. Lay treasure up in Heaven by investing your resources into the future eternity of others. Invest your life into the things of God. You cannot serve God and money. When the light breaks through to eternity, where will your future be?

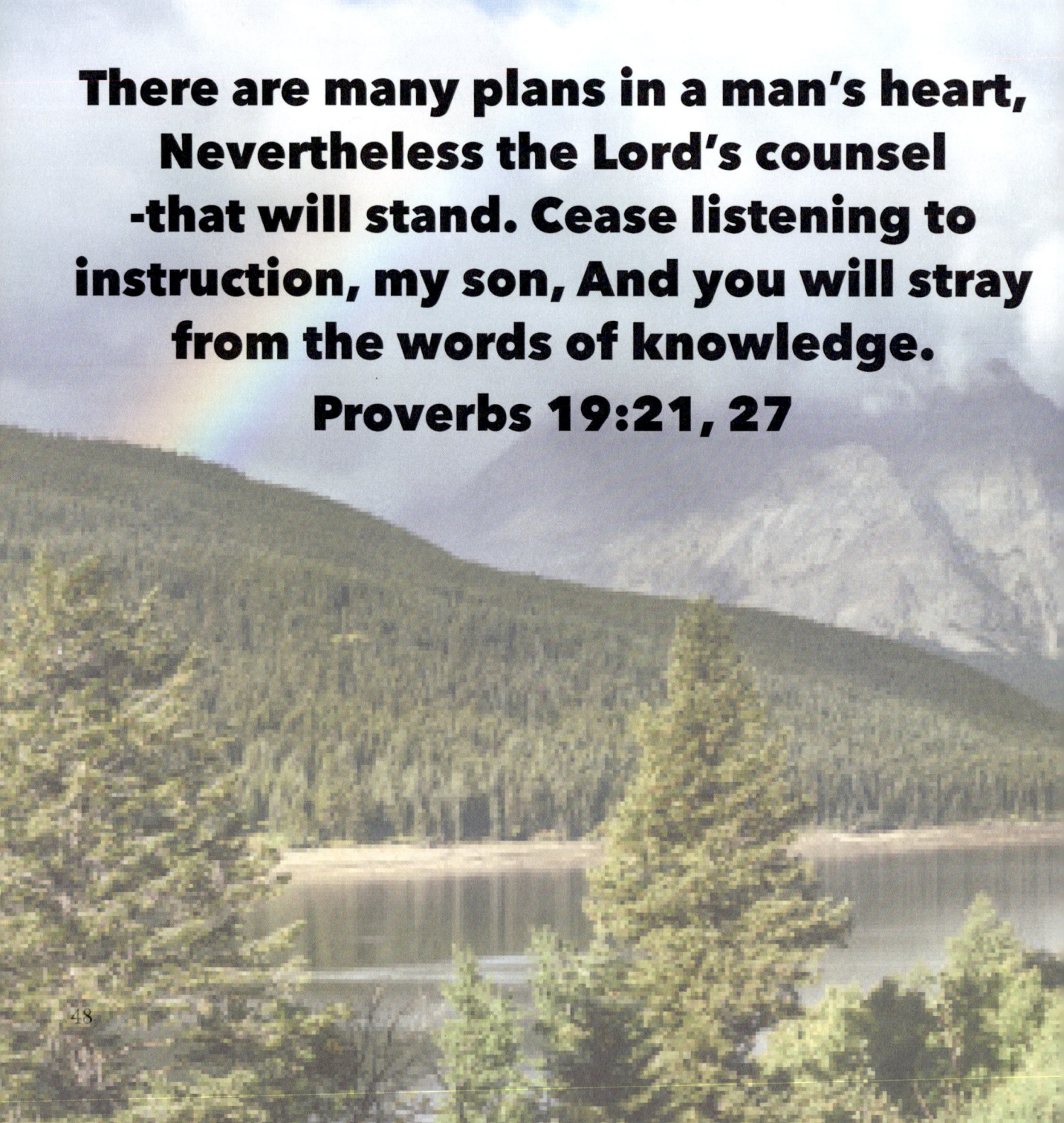

There are many plans in a man's heart, Nevertheless the Lord's counsel -that will stand. Cease listening to instruction, my son, And you will stray from the words of knowledge.

Proverbs 19:21, 27

Cease to Stray

Planning is important and guides oneself to accomplishment but a plan without the Lord's counsel will not be as filling and may be full of failures. God's instructions are there for a reason. He doesn't give instructions/laws to pull them back. A rainbow is for His promise to not flood the whole earth again...it does not mean He will permit sin. This country as a nation has ceased listening to God and has gone its own way encouraging sin at the highest levels of government and enacting laws against God from the murder of children to the abominations of lifestyles that defile the innocent. Do not expect our country's slogan "one nation under God" to stand, for the foundations of such are already torn out. This government cannot save itself nor anyone else. Nevertheless... love this word.... the Lord's counsel (advice, wisdom, word) THAT will stand. He is unchanging. Don't be fooled by churches whose standards do not line up with God to stand. The days are becoming more fraught, and the truth has been painted with so many lies that it is hard to perceive what is...nevertheless! Nevertheless-in spite of all, God's plan has not changed. The rainbow is still His promise and not a painted falsehood that others take to distort truth. His promises still stand, and His faithfulness is still there for those who walk in His counsel. The government cannot stop a rainbow from appearing where God wants it to appear, nor can they hide nor distort His truth from those who seek His counsel. Worried about the future? Seek His counsel and not that of others. Nevertheless....in contrast to all that man does.... God's counsel will stand! Not the report of the doctor nor the rules of a government hiding the truth for they only see through a glass darkly...cancer cannot control God, CoVid doesn't control God, nothing controls God...not even crooked, lying religious leaders...what does God say? No weapon formed shall prosper. What does God say about His plans for you? I know the plans I have for you...Jeremiah 29:11! Remember this word no matter what happens.... Nevertheless!!! God wins! Jesus is coming soon!!! His promises still stand! Great is His faithfulness! I'm still in His hands-this is my confidence! He has and will never fail!

For as the heavens are high above the earth, So great is His mercy toward those who fear Him; As far as the east is from the west, So far has He removed our transgressions from us. As a father pities his children, So the Lord pities those who fear Him.
For He knows our frame; He remembers that we are dust. As for man, his days are like grass; As a flower of the field, so he flourishes. For the wind passes over it, and it is gone, And its place remembers it no more. But the mercy of the Lord is from everlasting to everlasting On those who fear Him, And His righteousness to children's children,

Psalms 103:11-17

50

Caught Up

Sometimes it is easy to get caught up in the immediate concerns or troubles of life. Many times, our mind becomes consumed with our immediate problems, and we become overwhelmed and forget to acknowledge His goodness in our life. He knows us. Our time on this earth is but a whisper of eternity and yet He takes time to care for our smallest needs if we but ask. When I first read this part about a father pities his children...I was confused because pity to me meant felt sorry for...but in this it means has empathy for...feels their needs...this verse states that the Creator of all the universe feels the needs of those who respect His authority. Wow! His mercy to us is as boundless as the light years of space. He removes our sins permanently and fully. Oh, that we would grasp this and refresh ourselves with this. He knows our failures, our wants, our needs, our concerns. He created us in our mother's womb and knows us in the minutest detail. David said in this Psalms that man is like a grass as far as his days but flourishing like a flower. Our time here is limited but fragrant. What fragrance of your life will linger when you are gone? The Lord's fragrance is a garden of flowers constantly reproducing so that the scent of His presence is constant. Look around you. Inhale His fragrance in those whom He refreshes. His mercies are forever. Your children's children...your legacy...is it one of the fragrances of mercy? Is it filled with His love & joy? These problems you are having now are fleeting but your reaction to them is your fragrance to those around you that last. What scent are you passing on to those around you?

Lord, I ask that the fragrance of your love, mercy, joy, and forgiveness be the smell that permeates my life. Lord, let my words heal a heart that hurts. Let my life be a sacrifice to you. Let me be broken and spilled out for you so that your fragrance is all others smell and perceive when they see me. Wrap me in a cloak of your love. Help me to be your hands extended.

Jesus said to her, "I am the resurrection and the life. He who believes in Me, though he may die, he shall live. And whoever lives and believes in Me shall never die. Do you believe this?"

John 11:25-26

Do You Believe This?

This is a rock formation in Arizona called the "Eye of God" and yet while it is a thing of beauty, we know that God's eye is not limited to this one location nor to only the people who go to see it. Jesus isn't limited to a time, place or person but is the resurrection and life to all who believe in Him. The outcasts of society to the strongest moral man are all subject to the same question He posed that day so long ago.. "Do you believe this?" What do you have to believe in order to have the God of all creation see you as the Apple of His eye? That whoever believes in Him, though he may die on this earth will live eternal in glory! That's shouting grounds! Better than a touchdown! This is the best play ever! He didn't just score the winning point; He won the whole game with one play! To get on that winning team requires signing up through a simple confession...yes, Lord, I believe that You, the creator of all eternity are the Lord of my life! I accept you as my Savior and will walk with you in confidence until the end of this journey...such a simple confession with amazing benefits, better than millions of dollars in a contract...you win 🏅 you earn the reward of Heaven for eternity just by allowing Him to rule your life. Not a government mandate but a loving Savior! What a wonderful day! Yes Lord, I believe in You!

But what does it say? "The word is near you, in your mouth and in your heart" (that is, the word of faith which we preach): that if you confess with your mouth the Lord Jesus and believe in your heart that God has raised Him from the dead, you will be saved. For with the heart one believes unto righteousness, and with the mouth confession is made unto salvation.

Romans 10:8-10

Near Enough

The Word, not "a" word. The Word in John 1 states that The Word is synonymous with Jesus! "In the beginning was the word and the word was with God and the word was God."So let's look again, The word (Jesus) is near you, in your mouth and in your heart. Grab this! It's really good if you get it. The Word of Faith (you are acting with Jesus' power of attorney) lives in you! Get it! You have the power in the name of Jesus! It takes you acting in faith! Why can one believe in faith that God has raised Jesus from the dead so that you can be saved but not believe He lives in you and is able to command storms to cease, people to be healed, situations to be resolved, and mountains to be moved? The same God who raised Jesus from the grave lives in us if we have confessed that we believe through our heart and our mouth. Here's a question: are you walking in mountain moving faith or only pebble kicking faith? God not only can but He will work in you and through you! Join me...let's testify to His mountain moving faith in your life! What has God done through you lately? What mountain has He moved? What storms has He calmed? When you begin to testify to His goodness and see where He has brought you from to where you are today....you will once again know the reason why you love Him so much....the old song says "You can take the world, it's wealth and fortunes, I don't need earth's fame, for it's my desire to live for Him" and that's the key! So, what does it say? Jesus is near you! Jesus is in your mouth which means you speak, and the winds/waves obey! Jesus is in your heart, so He guides your choices! #mountainmovingfaith #TheWordIsJesus let's testify to His goodness!

And Jesus answered and said to them: "Take heed that no one deceives you. For many will come in My name, saying, 'I am the Christ,' and will deceive many. And you will hear of wars and rumors of wars. See that you are not troubled; for all these things must come to pass, but the end is not yet. For nation will rise against nation, and kingdom against kingdom. And there will be famines, pestilences, and earthquakes in various places. All these are the beginning of sorrows. "Then they will deliver you up to tribulation and kill you, and you will be hated by all nations for My name's sake. And then many will be offended, will betray one another, and will hate one another. Then many false prophets will rise up and deceive many. And because lawlessness will abound, the love of many will grow cold. But he who endures to the end shall be saved. And this gospel of the kingdom will be preached in all the world as a witness to all the nations, and then the end will come.

Matthew 24:4-14

Rumors

Matthew 24 tells us of the end of days, and I have broken into pieces for ease of reading. The first part tells us that we will know we are in the last days when there are wars and rumors of wars with nations rising against nation, then famine, pestilence, and earthquakes in diverse places. But that is not the end... false prophets must first rise up and the true Christian who stands for the truth will be hated by many...this is a sign...we are in these end times. Jesus is coming soon! The signs of the times are everywhere. History tells us of many false prophets, wars, earthquakes, and scripture warns us that just like the days of Noah, people will be consumed with self and unaware that the time has come. But the one who endures to the end will be saved. The generation of people who saw Israel become a nation in 1948 is growing older and God said that that generation would not pass away until His return. He's coming soon!

That Christ may dwell in your hearts through faith; that you, being rooted and grounded in love, may be able to comprehend with all the saints what is the width and length and depth and height– to know the love of Christ which passes knowledge; that you may be filled with all the fullness of God. Now to Him who is able to do exceedingly abundantly above all that we ask or think, according to the power that works in us, to Him be glory in the church by Christ Jesus to all generations, forever and ever. Amen.
Ephesians 3:17-21

Grounded

Rooted and grounded in faith and the love of God is the only way we can comprehend His love for us and the world. The fullness of God is only known through the faith to know that He is able to do EXCeedingly Abundantly above what we think or ask. The measure of God's love for us is beyond our comprehension in depth, height, width, and length. It is higher than the heavens, deeper than the seas, wider than the horizons and longer than the distance through the Milky Way. Our mind is not able to manage the sheer amount of His love. Just imagine the most love you can and know it is more!

For the word of God is living and powerful, and sharper than any two-edged sword, piercing even to the division of soul and spirit, and of joints and marrow, and is a discerner of the thoughts and intents of the heart.
Hebrews 4:12

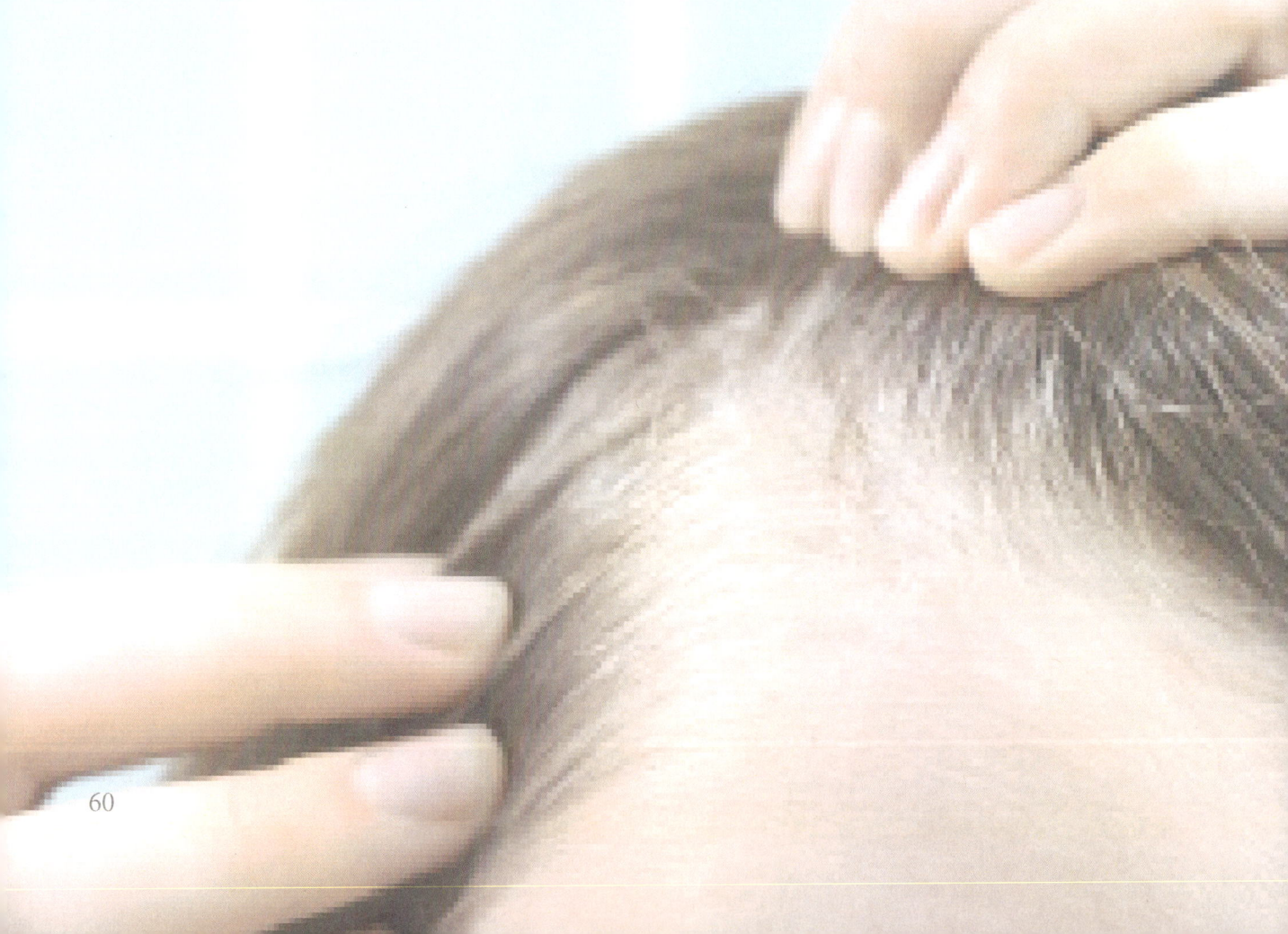

Living Word

God's word is living...breathing...active in our lives but only if we put the ingredients into the mix. Yeast is a small powerful fungus that can wreak havoc on someone's system or be the wonderful tool to produce bread! It's all about how it is used in the body/baking etc. My point is that, as I say, looking at my hair loss this morning, it put me in tears! Then I remembered the grace of my mother when she went through hair loss due to her cancer. As I shaved her head, she sang "I'm going on...." so I choose to be like my momma...I'm not going to let a spinal surgery and hair loss define me...I'm choosing to activate the power of God's word in my life, dividing my soul/spirit from the physical outlook of this body. I'm laying my treasures up. I will not let a loss of hair, feeling in my body or pain define me! I am a child of God, royalty, a princess from the Highest Court and I intend to be what He has for me! No matter what comes my way, I'm going on towards His mark of the High calling because Jesus is coming soon!

"If you love those who love you, what credit is that to you? Even sinners love those who love them. And if you do good to those who are good to you, what credit is that to you? Even sinners do that. And if you lend to those from whom you expect repayment, what credit is that to you? Even sinners lend to sinners, expecting to be repaid in full. But love your enemies, do good to them, and lend to them without expecting to get anything back. Then your reward will be great, and you will be children of the Most High, because he is kind to the ungrateful and wicked. Be merciful, just as your Father is merciful.

Judging Others

"Do not judge, and you will not be judged. Do not condemn, and you will not be condemned. Forgive, and you will be forgiven. Give, and it will be given to you. A good measure, pressed down, shaken together and running over, will be poured into your lap. For with the measure you use, it will be measured to you."
He also told them this parable: "Can the blind lead the blind? Will they not both fall into a pit? The student is not above the teacher, but everyone who is fully trained will be like their teacher. "Why do you look at the speck of sawdust in your brother's eye and pay no attention to the plank in your own eye? How can you say to your brother, 'Brother, let me take the speck out of your eye,' when you yourself fail to see the plank in your own eye? You hypocrite, first take the plank out of your eye, and then you will see clearly to remove the speck from your brother's eye.

A Tree and Its Fruit

"No good tree bears bad fruit, nor does a bad tree bear good fruit. Each tree is recognized by its own fruit. People do not pick figs from thorn bushes, or grapes from briers. A good man brings good things out of the good stored up in his heart, and an evil man brings evil things out of the evil stored up in his heart. For the mouth speaks what the heart is full of.

The Wise and Foolish Builders

"Why do you call me, 'Lord, Lord,' and do not do what I say? As for everyone who comes to me and hears my words and puts them into practice, I will show you what they are like. They are like a man building a house, who dug down deep and laid the foundation on rock. When a flood came, the torrent struck that house but could not shake it, because it was well built. But the one who hears my words and does not put them into practice is like a man who built a house on the ground without a foundation. The moment the torrent struck that house, it collapsed and its destruction was complete.

Luke 6:32-49

A Lot

I know, I know., it's a lot of scripture this morning but I woke this morning with "written in red" on my heart. Letters of mercy...God wrote His love...on a hillside so long, long ago...there were 3 hillsides of significance, as He sat before the multitude performing miracles and teaching, the hillside of Golgotha where he wrote his eternal love in crimson, & the hillside where He ascended and will return...these letters of red are His words to us. Such rich advice that is hard for us to fathom, grasp and incorporate in our lives. So, I divided it up for you & me. One set each hour today or each day through next week...this is just a portion of His sermon...like my pastor Ray Holman...Jesus taught a series but His lasted for hours through a day rather than once per week...start with Blessed are those who are poor...& think He came as a baby, lowly in a manger...He came to the poor and downtrodden for a reason! He came there because the love of money is rooted in evil. He said blessed are the poor, the hungry, the heartbroken and the reviled for they will rejoice...it is eternal Hope. I had someone ask me this week why I was so upbeat and energetic when I have such pain and a scary, major surgery before me...I told her...because this world isn't my home...my hope isn't in my body or any one thing or person, but my hope is built on nothing less than Letters written in RED!

But whoever keeps His word, truly the love of God is perfected in him. By this we know that we are in Him. He who says he abides in Him ought himself also to walk just as He walked.

I John 2:5-6

He Was And Is

He was the word in the beginning, and He still is. What a wonderful God He is. By this we know we are in Him...we walk as He walked. The fad WWJD was around when I was growing up, but it shouldn't be a fad to walk in What Would Jesus Do? it should be our lifestyle. C.S. Lewis penned an allegory called The Lion, the Witch and The Wardrobe which became a famous movie, and many missed the point. He was trying to tell us that walking with God is as simple as believing as a child in the magic of a portal to another world. Scripture tells us that we walk in spiritual planes where principalities not of this world are at work and yet we fail to see them because our eyes get caught up in the natural of what we feel. Jairus' daughter was ill and near death, so he came to Jesus seeking her healing but as he arrived a servant came and told him she had died. He still approached Jesus saying Lord, my daughter is sick, and my servant says she's dead, but I believe you can heal her and please help my un-belief. That's a paraphrase of what he said but the point is to realize that he recognized his unbelief and prayed to God to help him with it.

The woman with the issue of blood was not supposed to be around people but she knew if she could just reach the hem of His garment she could be healed and when she touched it, Jesus felt her faith and stated that Her faith made her whole. Elijah's servant could only see the enemy surrounding them until Elijah, through God's power, removed the scales from his eyes to see the supernatural at work. The point here is that if we abide in Him, we should walk, talk, and act in the supernatural faith that these who have gone before us demonstrate to us. We see only the natural and get caught up in the natural failing to walk in the supernatural! Science and meds blind us to His ways. We walk in the pain and the doctor's reports but fail to realize that God is working as The Great Physician and there is nothing too big or too little for Him. Does He use doctors? Yes, he absolutely does! Lord, you know me more intimately than anyone. You know my strengths and my weaknesses. You know I believe but the Lord helps my unbelief...heal my body, take away this pain. Touch the bones, sinews, and nerves. Make me like you. Lord, today I reach out in faith to touch the hem of your garment in faith believing that I will be healed. I believe. These mountains in my life will be moved by the power in the name of Jesus!

You're blessed when you stay on course, walking steadily on the road revealed by God. You're blessed when you follow his directions, doing your best to find him. That's right— you don't go off on your own; you walk straight along the road he set.

You, God, prescribed the right way to live; now you expect us to live it. Oh, that my steps might be steady, keeping to the course you set; Then I'd never have any regrets in comparing my life with your counsel.

I thank you for speaking straight from your heart; I learn the pattern of your righteous ways. I'm going to do what you tell me to do; don't ever walk off and leave me.

Psalm 119:1-8

GPS

GPS is an interesting tool especially when you are in an area you are unfamiliar with, and it directs you to drive in what feels like circles! Unlike GPS, which is manmade and often faulty, God's direction is not an off-course experience, but He can sometimes take you through a lesson again or reroute you because of decisions you've made to go off course. God prescribes our path because He knows us more intimately than we know ourselves but when we get off course in our spirit and "squirrel" off to catch the shiny new nut or bauble or fad...He gently directs us through our experiences to get back on track. There is a pattern to His counsel and direction which we must learn and by doing so we are blessed. Does this mean that when I go through hardships that God has left me or is teaching me a lesson? Well, He never leaves us nor forsakes us but if we wander off the path of His direction...just like a GPS, He must reroute us to get us back on the right way and sometimes that rerouting is a journey in itself that we must learn from. When you are going through a struggle and wondering where God is...simply reach out and say: Lord, reroute me to your path. Give me your wisdom as I journey this side road or rocky path to the place you are leading me. Lord, I am eager to be led by the still waters and lie down in the green pastures once again, so please take me through this valley of the shadow of death safely. Give me your peace and your strength in all things. I know you are guiding me and Jesus, just take the wheel here and get me back to your path. Wanna know how I am doing...i am Rerouting....learning the pattern of my Savior.

Come to Me, all you who labor and are heavy laden, and I will give you rest.
Take My yoke upon you and learn from Me, for I am gentle and lowly in heart, and you will find rest for your souls.
Matthew 11:28-29

Heavy Rest

Rest. What a concept. My staff & my husband have done everything in their power to encourage me to rest. My mind is busy even when my body fails me. I got that from my mother, Teresa, who never stops. In fact, she cracked me up this past week when I told her the doctor said this back thing was genetic and I said it was from her because she always says her back hurts...and she has fire in her arms/legs...she told me this past week that she was healthy cause all she had was a little cancer once (stage 4-very serious...but God)! Anyway, the point is rest. Our burdens are not something we must bear alone. He gives complete peace. When mom had cancer and was doing chemo, Domonique interviewed her and she said, Peace isn't the absence of the storm but rather complete confidence in Him who controls the storm. I feel this. If God brought me to this, He has a plan and I can trust it more than I can trust my husband to care for me (which he's amazing!!!), more than I can trust my staff to care for our business (which is complete because I'm just small potatoes to these incredible people), more than I can trust my parents who will be bombarding heaven for me along with their church, my church & my pastors...the point is that I trust God completely. His ways aren't mine and His purpose is higher, so I give my burdens to Him, and I've joined yoke with Him because He carries me. Father, today I give you all of me. I give you all my burdens, both seen and unseen. I give you any anxiety and stress hidden from my consciousness. I give you this broken body and this active mind. I give you all I am to all I know. I will give it to your safe keeping. As the songwriter says, " I don't know about tomorrow, I just live from day to day. I don't borrow from the sunshine for the skies may turn grey. I don't worry over the future for I know what Jesus said and today He walks beside me for He knows what is ahead. Many things about tomorrow I don't seem to understand but I know who holds tomorrow and I know He holds my hand!" I trust in You God. You are my hiding place and shelter from life's storms. I will learn from you and rest in you.

She that dwells in the secret place of the Most High will live peacefully under the shadow of the Almighty. I will say of the LORD, He is my refuge and my fortress: My God; in him will I trust. He shall cover me with his feathers, and under his wings I will trust:
His truth shall be my shield
and buckler.
For he shall give his angels charge over me, To keep me in all my ways.

Psalm 91:1-2, 4, 11

Prepare the Heart

As I began to prepare my heart and mind today for surgery, I started by personalizing some of my favorite scriptures and writing them upon my heart. There is something that happens when the Word becomes alive in you. It quickens your mortal body...it lives and breathes in you. It rises up to do exactly what scripture says. He answers you! He hears you! He feels you and calms you. His perfect peace settles on you like a warm blanket. Going through this season I have had my "Even If" moments for sure. I asked Him to move this mountain. I prayed His will be done despite mine and I meant it. But I am confident that He who began a good work in me is faithful to complete it. Today is a big day for me. The surgery is at noon. Even now as I type, I cannot feel my hands and feet, so I know it is time. I believe this mountain is moving today. I believe that things are changing. I believe. I know Him intimately and what He says He will do, He will do. He is The Word and has been from the beginning and He is Alpha and Omega. My friend David McMillan always says "If today was your very last day on Earth, who would you call and what would you say? Why are you waiting? Make the call." Today is not promised to any of us. But He is our refuge. He has been faithful all my days and I will trust in Him. Lord, into your hands I give my fears and failures. I give thanks for all my blessings and successes. To you today I give my spirit and soul and body. I trust you to walk with me through these challenges ahead. Be with my family, friends, and colleagues today. Hold them close to you. I bless you Lord for your faithfulness, and I will rest today in you.

Be assured that from the first day we heard of you, we haven't stopped praying for you, asking God to give you wise minds and spirits attuned to his will, and so acquire a thorough understanding of the ways in which God works.
We pray that you'll live well for the Master, making him proud of you as you work hard in his orchard. As you learn more and more how God works, you will learn how to do your work.
We pray that you'll have the strength to stick it out over the long haul - not the grim strength of gritting your teeth but the glory-strength God gives. It is strength that endures the unendurable and spills over into joy,
thanking the Father who makes us strong enough to take part in everything bright and beautiful that he has for us.
God rescued us from dead-end alleys and dark dungeons. He's set us up in the kingdom of the Son he loves so much,
the Son who got us out of the pit we were in, got rid of the sins we were doomed to keep repeating.

Colossians 1:9-14

Adventures

It's beeeeeeen an adventure! Still ongoing, but yet...this verse spoke to me today, the truth that so many of us failed to realize, and yet, it is the beauty of the gospel in our lives. So, thank you from the bottom of my heart. Thank you for praying and sharing our burdens.

The long/short is that this body of mine is not always playing the melody as God intends it to do so in our bodies. So many struggle with this same issue, from chronic illness to surgical issues. We are all but vessels and some have weaknesses. Praying for one another is key to growth and working in this orchard of His. Sticking it out for the duration requires that we hold one another up in good and bad. This is how we learn more and more how God works. It isn't grim strength, but God's glory strength. This is what endures the unendurable and spills over into joy. God rescued us from the depth and the dire places of doom and despair to give us life abundant. This is what makes us strong enough to endure the depths of despair for that which is bright and beautiful.

God can pour on the blessings in astonishing ways so that you're ready for anything and everything, more than just ready to do what needs to be done. As one psalmist puts it, He throws caution to the winds, giving to the needy in reck- less abandon. His right-living, right-giving ways never run out, never wear out. This most generous God who gives seed to the farmer that becomes bread for your meals is more than extravagant with you. He gives you something you can then give away, which grows into full-formed lives, robust in God, wealthy in every way, so that you can be generous in every way, producing with us great praise to God.

2 Corinthians 9:8-11

All Knowing

Talking with my family about the blessings of knowing He is working through others around us. It is powerful to know that the God who knows all, sees all and is all, gives in abandon to us in the way we need it before we even know it. As the psalmists put it, He gives to us in reckless abandon. His right-living, right-giving ways never run out. This is the most generous God who pours His blessings out in astonishing ways upon us so that we are ready for anything and everything. More than just barely ready to do what needs to be done. Generous living breeds blessing and grows into robust, fully formed lives. Be the seed that will become the bread for others around you.

Therefore, having been justified by faith, we have peace with God through our Lord Jesus Christ, through whom also we have access by faith into this grace in which we stand, and rejoice in hope of the glory of God. And not only that, but we also glory in tribulations, knowing that tribulation produces perseverance; and perseverance, character; and character, hope. Now hope does not disappoint, because the love of God has been poured out in our hearts by the Holy Spirit who was given to us.

Romans 5:1-5

Focus

When I focus on where I was to where I am, things look a lot better. When I focus on the pain, I get bogged into it. The point is this body is aging and time is what it takes to recover...heal. Focused mindset can change perspective.

As I read this morning, my mind focused on the word tribulation. What is the purpose of tribulations, which are long-time trials? The purpose is here...it's to work perseverance because perseverance brings character and character brings hope. If our Hope is built on nothing less than Jesus' love & righteousness, then it is steadfast. The foundation on which we build our lives is that Jesus Christ is the I AM. We have access to perfect peace because we are justified or made clean through faith in the grace He has bestowed upon us. In a nutshell, we can stand and celebrate because He has withstood it all for us. By His stripes we are healed, through His resurrection we are made new, by His atonement we are forgiven, through His grace we are saved.... over and over, it comes back to the basics of while we were so caught up in ourselves, He sacrificially gave himself as a spotless Lamb through His love for us. It all boils down to the fact that while we are yet sinners, Christ loved us so much that He willingly gave up His throne in glory and became man so He might experience what we experience and go a step further to save us from ourselves. Wow! That's amazing love!

"You are the salt of the earth; but if the salt loses its flavor, how shall it be seasoned? It is then good for nothing but to be thrown out and trampled underfoot by men. "You are the light of the world. A city that is set on a hill cannot be hidden. Nor do they light a lamp and put it under a basket, but on a lampstand, and it gives light to all who are in the house. Let your light so shine before men, that they may see your good works and glorify your Father in heaven.

Matthew 5:13-16

Salt n Light

Salt and Light. Recently my pastor shared a series (he's good at those) on being the Salt and Light. It's amazing how many purposes Salt has which gives us guidance on how we are to be used of God in today's world. I encourage you to go to Bethel Assembly of God Shreveport FB page and view these sermons. This morning I was thinking about salt, and its uses in the body since my body has been through a thing or two lately. Then God spoke to me about purpose and how His divine purpose is working despite my situation and through it. Being sick is emotionally exhausting on so many around me. I hate being needy and I have no choice right now. How can I possibly be light to others when my light is struggling to stay bright? Scripture gives us this answer. Let your light shine...it doesn't describe the brightness but rather just says let it shine. My wavering light is able to be seen in a dark night whether I'm on the hilltop or in the valley.

In fact, when your light is flickering in a valley, it draws more attention than on a hilltop in a city because it stands out. Being real and staying lit with His word allows others in the valleys to see direction and as lights connect, the brightness comes. Honestly, I do not struggle with the Why so much as the How Long? And I can truthfully say that my light burns on the oil of God's word so it will stay lit even in rough patches. Yes, this is a valley of pain and uncertainty, but it is also a time of sweet anointing and blessings. Lord, I come to you right now hurting in my body. My spirit is tired and weak, but I know you are strong, and you are my strength and my fortress. Today I run to you and ask you to hold me. Lift me, light me so I can be used of you despite this valley. Guide me with your presence today. Make me salt and light.

Be anxious for nothing, but in everything by prayer and supplication, with thanksgiving, let your requests be made known to God;

Philippians 4:6

Anxiety

Wow! What a statement...Be anxious for nothing...just let your requests be made known to God in prayer and supplication with Thanksgiving. How hard it is to simply rest in Him. I'm a control freak, I'll admit it. It's infinitely challenging to turn things over to others but sometimes there is no choice or it is the best choice. This season of my life has been learning this lesson...that I cannot control all and I have to learn to turn loose. The hardest thing to turn loose of is the thing I have no true control over anyway. It's me. I'm a worrier. I do trust God but (I know there shouldn't be a but) But...I'm a worrier because I care about the details. I don't worry about the big things because I understand God has those...

I worry about the dogs being out too late or everything being in place. In other words, I have some anxiety. I'm sure I drive Wes & my boys nuts with it but it's me...however, I will say when I'm sick...the details don't matter as much. The last few days have been hard...my gut is still torn up and my back well, it's healing but sore. My spirit has just been tired. Not down, just tired. So, when this verse popped up today, I know God was reminding me that He has this and it's time for me to say, ok. God, I understand you're with me and you've got this. Lift me up Lord into your arms and let me rest there anxious for nothing.

God has gone up with a shout, The Lord with the sound of a trumpet. Sing praises to God, sing praises! Sing praises to our King, sing praises! For God is the King of all the earth; Sing praises with understanding. God reigns over the nations; God sits on His holy throne. The princes of the people have gathered together, The people of the God of Abraham. For the shields of the earth belong to God; He is greatly exalted.

Psalms 47:5-9

Got It

I'll always remember the first time I "got" basketball. I was in college cheering, but I didn't really understand the principles behind the game. I was more concerned with what I was doing, but Liese Thompson decided to explain the game. She wasn't a big sports avarice in my thinking, but she explained it in such a way that I got it. It became more than a game of putting a ball in a net, and the mechanics became more. Now as I'm older, I've cheered for many a team for multiple reasons, but I have yet to see the people of God get as excited as the fans on a winning team watching a ball go down a court or field. In this verse, I see the phrase "sing praises with understanding" and I think that is the missing piece.

We still don't get it...we are lost in the game, haphazardly cheering, never realizing that the God of all creation reigns over all and we are His people with all of the benefits of the win. Today is a day of celebration no matter what circumstances you are in because He is God, and we are on the winning team. The challenges have been met and the price has been paid. The ball went into the basket for the winning point. Time to cheer in excitement and joy for He has conquered all. Lord, I sing praises to your name...I shout in joy for you are above all and you have won! I sing with understanding that you have all things under you and through you all things are new. Shout to the Lord!

Now we exhort you, brethren, warn those who are unruly, comfort the fainthearted, uphold the weak, be patient with all. See that no one renders evil for evil to anyone, but always pursue what is good both for yourselves and for all. Rejoice always, pray without ceasing, in everything give thanks; for this is the will of God in Christ Jesus for you. Do not quench the Spirit. Do not despise prophecies. Test all things; hold fast what is good.
Abstain from every form of evil.

1 Thessalonians 5:14-22

Tall Order!

Warn, comfort, uphold, and be patient. Wow! Tall orders. And that's just the beginning. This is a list of the things to live a Godly life. In the middle of it all is my mom's favorite verse, which is, rejoice always and in everything give thanks. How does one do all these things without becoming overwhelmed? Praying without ceasing...prayer is an ongoing conversation with God...it never stops, it may pause for a few minutes but the constant Interactional wave is the drive behind the other parts. Prayer promotes intimacy because it is a constant. How does one grow close to another...intimacy, constant companionship, sharing of your most special thoughts and dreams and ideas...hearing the other person's heart and longing to spend time worshiping them, exalting them, and promoting them. Intimacy with God is achieved by spending time with Him, in His word, in Prayer, in constant communication. All the other parts become the what you do because of the love you have for the One. Rejoice, pray, give thanks...test, hold fast, and abstain...all a part of the mix...all comes from intimacy with God.

Then Jesus spoke to them again, saying, "I am the light of the world. He who follows Me shall not walk in darkness, but have the light of life."

John 8:12

What is the Light of Life?

Jesus said He is the Light of this world...and if we follow after Him, we shall not walk in darkness...but have the Light of Life. So, what is the Light of Life? Is it peace? Is it safety? Is it certainty?

Last night it was pitch black outside as it is only in the country, and I let the dogs out to take care of business. Once they got beyond the light of the porch, I could no longer see them, but I could still hear them barking, until I couldn't. I called and they didn't come, but I could hear coyotes in the area, so my heart triple timed as fear for my small dogs against a group of unseen predators arose. Then I saw the glowing eyes in the dark...I heard the little tinkle of the rabies tag against the collar and suddenly the fear was gone as the cute little pups sat at my feet waiting to come in. They never experienced the fear I had in my throat, for they could see the light and knew I was waiting for them. Their adventures were just a moment for them and a whole different experience for me. The Light of Life is Eternal Hope...you see, Jesus stands waiting in the Light for us to wander back into the fold.

He has the light on, he beckons and calls us home. Sometimes the world may seem dark and bleak but all we must do is look to Him, for He stands at the door with the Light on waiting for us to come home. The Light of Life is the Eternal Hope of Glory. He has gone before us to prepare the place for us, that where He is we may be for all eternity...The Light of Life beckons to us to come home out of the darkness of this world. Come Home...all who are living out in the dangers of this world full of predators seeking whom they may devour...isn't it time you turned toward the Light and ran Home? Lord, I am so thankful that despite all my adventures you have always got the Light of Life shining and beckoning me Home. Help me to be a light in the darkness as you are....

Rejoice in the Lord always.
Again I will say, rejoice! Let your gentleness be known to all men. The Lord is at hand. Be anxious for nothing, but in everything by prayer and supplication, with thanksgiving, let your requests be made known to God; and the peace of God, which surpasses all understanding, will guard your hearts and minds through Christ Jesus.

Philippians 4:4-7

Rejoice

Woke up this morning with this verse on my heart...have had a continuous message for the last few weeks of being anxious for nothing and rejoicing no matter the circumstances, as well as, the message of God's peace being supreme. Then I read it again. You see. I had read the familiar parts easily, but I left off two very important parts stuck in the middle. "Let your gentleness be known to all men. The Lord is at hand." I honestly had to ponder these today. I get letting my requests be known to God...I'm actually like a rockstar at that! And the peace of God reigning over me has been a super blessing these past weeks. Long story short, I went for a walk this afternoon with Wes, as I must do many times per day, but this particular time, some hurtful words were thrown at me inadvertently and unintentionally by someone, which really hurt, since I feel like I'm doing all I can to just be...my spirit rose up so fast and the words on the tip of my tongue were ready to blast, then I felt the Lord at hand gently nudge me. Not His way. So I responded passively and walked on. My spirit healed quickly and I felt His soothing hand paint the words said away. I don't even remember what they were right now. The sting is gone because God was at hand and He stepped in to soothe me. Life isn't always easy and harsh words are often spoken carelessly by people never intentionally harming, but I am so glad that His gentleness was at hand and He cushioned the hurt and changed it to a lesson I had pondered all day. Lord, thank you for always being there for me in the big things and the small. Thank you for stepping up and allowing your spirit to take reign in my heart rather than harsh words. Most of all, thank you for painting over those words with your gentleness. Help me to be known for your gentleness and pure joy in you! Thank you for your peace which passes all understanding and guarding my heart and mind!

Let no corrupt word. proceed out of your mouth, but what is good.. for necessary edification, that it may impart grace to the hearers And do not grieve the Holy Spirit of God, by whom you were sealed for the day of redemption. Let all bitterness, wrath, anger, clamor, and evil speaking be put away from you, with all malice. And be kind to one another, tenderhearted, forgiving one another, even as God in Christ forgave you.

Ephesians 4:29-32

Ouch!

Got my hand slapped this morning or maybe it was my mouth figuratively. I've read this a thousand times without hearing it. Corrupt...used maliciously or for personal gain...so no twisting of meanings for personal gain... only that which is good for necessary growth of others...that's very convicting! This is a definite chat from God telling us that as we sit behind these screens typing our opinions and responding to others that we are to only respond and react in a way that brings about necessary growth to impart grace to those who hear us. No anger, no unnecessary noise, no bitterness, no speaking evil of others, and no hidden agendas...only what is written or said in love, grace, and kindness with a tender heart. That means before we write or speak, we need to pray for God to guide us, because our human nature definitely will override this. I mean how to respond in forgiveness remembering that God forgave us...must be guided by God. When I was growing up, my mom said, if you cannot say something nice, say nothing at all. I guess that's this scripture in a nutshell. Lord, forgive me for when I've failed to respond correctly or have led others astray with my responses in a situation. Forgive me Lord for failing to remember that you forgave me so that I might be able to share your light. Give me your wisdom and grace as I go through the day to be the light you've given me to be. Help me to remember to say only what's necessary and to say it in a tender hearted, grace guided word from you.

I will instruct you and teach you in the way you should go; I will guide you with My eye. Do not be like the horse or like the mule, Which have no understanding, Which must be harnessed with bit and bridle, Else they will not come near you. Many sorrows shall be to the wicked; But he who trusts in the Lord, mercy shall surround him. Be glad in the Lord and rejoice, you righteous; And shout for joy, all you upright in heart!

Psalms 32:8-11

Eye of God

Guided by the Eye of God. He says not to be like the horse or the mule. When I had just been married a few years, Wes took me aside and told me that I was a horse, and he was a mule. He told me that we were yoked together, and horses will work themselves into the ground without stopping, but mules stop when they are tired. He said God had sent him to slow me down and keep me steady. I understand this verse now. Do not be like the horse working oneself incessantly into the grave nor stubborn like a mule unwilling to bend unless harnessed with bit and bridle. Instead, be surrounded by God's mercy and trust in the Lord so that He may give you release. Rejoice and shout for joy!

Jesus answered, "Most assuredly, I say to you, unless one is born of water and the Spirit, he cannot enter the kingdom of God. That which is born of the flesh is flesh, and that which is born of the Spirit is spirit.

Do not marvel that I said to you, 'You must be born again.' The wind blows where it wishes, and you hear the sound of it, but cannot tell where it comes from and where it goes.
So is everyone who is born of the Spirit."

John 3:5-8

Born of Spirit

Born of the Spirit. I was 5 when I gave my heart to Jesus and was born again of the Spirit. I was 11 years old when I was filled with the Holy Ghost with the evidence of speaking in tongues. I can remember these two days as fragrantly and in such detail as I remember anything but that's not all. I grew up understanding who God was, but I was 18 before I knew who God is, and I fall more and more in love with Him as the days go by. Being born of the Spirit is different than receiving and using the gifts of the Spirit. The gifts of the Spirit are active within you when you allow The Spirit to lead. Those who know me, know my spirit and recognize it. As I've been recovering, my spirit has been quiet and God's spirit has ministered to me. I have grown in Him because I leaned into Him. When a person trusts they can lean in knowing confidently that they will benefit from the experience which is why the verse says that those who are born of the spirit and are led by the Spirit are like the wind. The wind of God fills you and changes your nature but you must yield that nature into His Spirit and trust Him to direct your path. Lord, today I choose again to be immersed in your presence and to have your Spirit dwell in me. Flow through me Holy Spirit.

For the earth will be filled With the knowledge of the glory of the Lord, As the waters cover the sea.
Habakkuk 2:14

Earth

It fascinates me that anyone could see all the beauty in a photo like this and not see it as the handiwork of an amazing creator. The whole earth is filled with the knowledge of the glory of God, yet many fail to recognize it. In fact, if you read this chapter in Habakkuk, you will see that the chapter is a warning...a vision to be written to admonish those who build their cities around bloodshed and sin. It is an admonition to all of us that the whole earth is groaning under the weight of sin that has corrupted. Scripture tells us that the rocks will cry out the glory of God in an audible voice if we fail to recognize His glory. This photo screams of the intense love of our Creator God for His creation. He loves us deeply and wholly. He wants us to know Him intimately. I lived on Caddo Lake for over 4 years and looked out to the beauty of His creation...the voices of nature calling out to the Creator... every detail in nature...every atom, molecule, creature...knows Him...as the waters cover the sea, so vast is the knowledge of His glory...isn't it time that we recognize the King of Glory for who He truly is?

Rajeesh is so talented in capturing the very essence of the glory of God on film.... look and see that God is good and His mercy endures for all time.

Watch for this - a virgin will get pregnant and bear a son; They will name him Emmanuel (Hebrew for "God is with us").
Matthew 1:23

Hustle

Immanuel...God with us! We too often forget in the hustle & bustle. No matter what the situation...God is with us if we abide in Him! Seasons come and go, but so often we get caught up in the decor, the gift giving, the party, and the celebration that we forget the real reason for that season. Experience takes over the purpose. We get caught in the hustle and bustle of the event and miss the why. Seasonal celebrations from Christmas to Easter get lost in the chaos of the culture and miss the purpose of the one who came.

"A voice was heard in Ramah, Lamentation, weeping, and great mourning, Rachel weeping for her children, Refusing to be comforted, Because they are no more."
Matthew 2:18

Anchored

Christmas is a time to celebrate the birth of our savior but for many it is also a time of mourning. The birth of Jesus brought about the death of thousands due to Herod's jealousy, rage, and malice. This picture of a tree growing In seemingly impossible circumstances reflects this. Life can come despite the lack of circumstances to support it if we are anchored and rooted in Him. A vast desert in our lives, a place of sorrow, grief over dreams shattered, etc. can become a place of victory and growth if we allow our place of hurt to become a seed. You see a seed must die to bring new life. It is broken and changed into what it will become. We have a choice. We can choose to allow that seed to become rank, bitter, moldy, and fill our desert place with bitterness. Or we can allow that hurt & disappointment to become a place of growth in impossible places but rooting deeply in The Living Water. Lord, thank you for your covering and grace in impossible situations. I thank you that I can bring my hurts & disappointments to you and allow that seed of hurt to become a fruitful tree rooted in your grace & mercy. Father, help me to take old hurts and pains and plant them deep into your presence so that I may be fruitful and grow in impossible circumstances. Thank you for the gift of your son & this season of remembrance.

But Mary kept all these things and pondered them in her heart.

Luke 2:19

Processing

      Pondering is my process. Stopping and thinking on things. Taking time to mull them over. Examining them and really relishing the meaning that is behind it. Mary had faith when God spoke to her through an angel that she would have a child..,she went through a whole pregnancy without a lot of support, traveled to a strange place, birthed her first child in a stable and then had a bunch of strangers show up telling her Angels had appeared telling them about her birthing a king. The shepherds were running around telling everyone, but Mary kept these things and pondered them in her heart. Mary had a most intimate relationship with the God of all creation and she cherished this close to her. Now, we have the same opportunity to have that intimacy with God... and we have His word that we can ponder in our hearts. Let's take a lesson from this sweet girl who willingly and faithfully carried our Savior in her womb...let's take the time this season to ponder all that He has said and done for us. Take time for Christ this year!

His name was called Jesus, the name given by the angel before He was conceived in the womb. "For my eyes have seen Your salvation Which You have prepared before the face of all peoples, A light to bring revelation to the Gentiles, And the glory of Your people Israel."

Luke 2:21, 30-32

The Promise

Filled with promise...Mary and Joseph were separately told to call Him Jesus before they knew the child. There is much debate about the sacredness of a child in the womb, but scripture tells us over and over how God knits us together in the quietness of the womb.

Simeon was told that before he died, he would see the salvation of Israel, and Anna, a widow woman was also told...both of these saw and testified to His birth at His dedication. A light was born to shine in the darkness of the circumstances and to reveal the evil in many. Jesus came as a babe that we might have life eternal. He knew He would suffer and die, and Mary was told at His dedication that His life wouldn't be easy and that meant hers would not be either.

The point is that on this Christmas Day, you should realize He knew your whole life before you were conceived, and He loves you with everlasting love. That's the message of Christmas...that God loved you so much He sent His son to die for you so you might have eternal life. Merry Christmas!

The Lord is my shepherd; I shall not want. He makes me to lie down in green pastures; He leads me beside the still waters. He restores my soul; He leads me in the paths of righteousness For His names sake.

Psalms 23:1-3

The Semicolon

The semicolon is a unique punctuation because it means see what is before as a related sentence .... The Lord is my shepherd therefore I shall not want. Want is a funny word because it has so many connotations. I want a pair of shoes, compared to my wants...David was writing from the perspective of a shepherd, stating that The Lord provides green pastures to feed and still waters to drink for His sheep. He also talked about how God led him in paths of righteousness as he knew from experience that sheep tend to wander and had need of a shepherd to keep them on the right path. But there's that semicolon again...He restores my soul...in other words, the leading on the path of righteousness is a portion of restoration. Just think for a moment of how God has brought you through and restored you.

This means a lot to me as my body is currently in the restoration process from my back surgery, and it is not easy, but as I walk through the process, I can look back and say..I'm better today than yesterday. Sometimes that's what it takes in life...restoration on the path of righteousness one step at a time to reach the still waters and green pastures. This world isn't an easy place to navigate but if you have your hand in the hand of the creator of all eternity and the one who can speak to the winds and storms so they obey...why worry? Lord, I am so grateful that I can simply reach out and know you are here with me in all things. Thank you for your faithfulness through all of life's trials and blessings. Thank you for the green pastures, the still waters, your guiding hand on the paths of righteousness and that I know all my wants are met before I even think to ask.

The king's heart is in the hand of the Lord, Like the rivers of water; He turns it wherever He wishes. Every way of a man is right in his own eyes, But the Lord weighs the hearts.
He who-follows righteousness and mercy Finds life, righteousness, and honor.
Proverbs 21:1-2

Blame Game

We often get caught up in blame especially on the part of our government but here Solomon explains that God controls the heart of those in authority. A good example of this is in Exodus where we see Moses explaining that God hardened Pharaoh's heart or in Genesis where we see Him dealing with different kings' hearts and throughout scripture, we see God changing situations by dealing with the hearts of kings. God weighs the hearts of men meaning He sees the motives behind what one does and those that follow righteousness and mercy find the gifts of such. The deeper part of this is you are either a man or woman after God's heart following in His path willing and successfully or you are subject to the whims of the world...but God is still in control either way as He can turn the tides with a word, an action, or a thought. Every knee will bow to God either willingly or subjectively.

Therefore let him who thinks he stands take heed lest he fall. No temptation has overtaken you except such as is common to man; but God is faithful, who will not allow you to be tempted beyond what you are able, but with the temptation will also make the way of escape, that you may be able to bear it.

I Corinthians 10:12-13

The Part

The first part of this letter to the Corinthian church is an admonition by Paul to learn from the lessons of the Israelites in the Old Testament. Then he says that God always provides a way of escape from any test/temptation that comes our way...that we may be able to bear it. I think of the horrible punishment put upon Jesus as he was flogged, made to carry that cross, then crucified. His words were not accusations but rather intercession as He said..Father forgive them...for they know not what they do....He is faithful in everything. When you've done all you know to do, then just stand in the power & faithfulness of our God for truly He knows. Lord, I am so grateful that as this year draws to a close, you knew me...you know my needs, my wants, my desires. I ask you today to help me to be faithful as you are faithful and to love as you love.

You will guide me with Your counsel, And afterward receive me to glory. Whom have I in heaven but You? And there is none upon earth that I desire besides You. My flesh and my heart fail; But God is the strength of my heart and my portion forever.

Psalms 73:24-26

Guided Counsel

In this chapter David is looking back over his life and lamenting that things seem so much easier for others as he looks at it through earthly eyes. He sees wealth and abundance and people living the high life which he mistakes for contentment and happiness. Then...He goes into the house of God and begins to worship. His vision is cleared, and his purpose is renewed. He then has the scales of discontent removed and he sees the jealousy and envy for what they are. He sees the pride and rot and complete degradation of those he had previously lamented that he wanted to be as...his eyes are open to spiritual things instead of mortal. I have never seen a life end or the passing of anyone that allows the carryover of things. Possessions are easy to be envious of, but they have no eternal consequences. Once David's eyes are opened, he pens the verses below. This should be our guiding wisdom as we close this year and head into 2022. God is our portion forever. His strength is ours; His counsel guides us and when the end comes, He will receive us to himself. What a promise! Lord, how can I say thanks for all the things you have done for me this year. Things so underserved yet you've given over and over to me. The voices of a million angels could not declare my gratitude. All that I am or ever hope to be, I owe it all to you!! To you God be the Glory...as the heavens declare it in the picture below...there is none like you!

Incline my heart to Your testimonies, And not to covetousness. Turn away my eyes from looking at worthless things, And revive me in Your way. Behold, I long for Your precepts; Revive me in Your righteousness. Remember the word to Your servant, Upon which You have caused me to hope. This is my comfort in my affliction, For Your word has given me life. you are my portion, O Lord; I have said that I would keep Your words.

Psalms 119:36-37, 40, 49-50, 57

Longest Chapter

Psalms 119 is the longest chapter in the Bible, and it contains the midpoint of the KJV Bible...but it is a collection of verses of David's song and it is about leaning in.

I read recently about when a lean-to was built, it only needed a couple of braces because its strength came from the house wall that it was braced into. Strong winds may buffet it and cause it to wobble or get off center but when that happens more bracing to the main house is added.

David is leaning into God's principles, precepts, and laws in this song because he doesn't get why it seems others have everything they want, and he struggles. He begins this song asking God to help him with his attitude of covetousness and end by delighting His soul in God. The key is leaning in. Leaning in means complete reliance upon. Immediately after this back surgery and for the last few weeks, I have experienced leaning in, utter dependence upon my husband. There are many things he has had to do for me in this time that I have never had to ask anyone to do for me..there have been moments of complete humiliation that he has raised me from by his gentle hands. This is the picture of leaning in. I trust Wes with all of me because he has had complete control and he has stood the test. God has always had my portion but somehow I segregated Him into sections of time/place in my life without intention. Leaning in to Wes has strengthened our marriage and relationship like nothing else and God gives us this example of marriage even calling us His bride so we can begin to understand that we must lean in to His strength, to His fortitude, to His constancy, to His wall of precepts. We are but a lean-to built against the strong wall of the house...as long as we lean into the house, we are braced by Him and anchored to Him. When the winds of life begin to buffet us, we can brace ourselves with His word and know that we have added another link to the source, strengthening who we are in Him. Lord, I am so very grateful for your word and I delight myself in your word daily. I confess, Lord, that I often box my time with you up and section it off and I repent of this. I am so sorry for my failure to recognize my need to lean in fully on you. Lord, pick me up with your strong frame and form my mind into your mold. Help me to lean in to you and not to allow the buffeting of life's storms to push me away but rather allow me to anchor in you and become stronger in your precepts as I learn to lean. Lord, you are my portion and I will no longer think of that as only a piece but rather you are my strong home. Lord I trust in you.

www.ingramcontent.com/pod-product-compliance
Lightning Source LLC
Chambersburg PA
CBRC090833120626
46547CB00009B/672